BRITAIN IN OLD  H S

READING
IN THE NEWS

SUE READ

SUTTON PUBLISHING LIMITED

Sutton Publishing Limited
Phoenix Mill · Thrupp · Stroud
Gloucestershire · GL5 2BU

First published 1998

Copyright © Sue Read, 1998

Title page: Engine derailed at Southcote
Junction, June 1949 (*see* p. 117).

British Library Cataloguing in Publication Data
A catalogue record for this book is available from the
British Library.

ISBN 0-7509-1474-2

Typeset in 10/12 Perpetua.
Typesetting and origination by
Sutton Publishing Limited.
Printed in Great Britain by
Ebenezer Baylis, Worcester.

To the Memory of Darby Allen

CONTENTS

An incident which attracted attention amid the bustle of life in Station Square on a March day in 1950.

INTRODUCTION

We need not justify the quality of excitement that the photograph has always had since its first use in a newspaper. It is the skill of the reporting photographer to capture the best documentary, dramatic and, on occasions, humorous picture. It is essential that each shot must be eye catching. However, as time passes a photograph becomes no longer just a visual representation of up-to-date news but a social document. We must look beyond the moment itself to the detail, whether it is fashion, mode of transport or general period style. Fifty years ago is well within living memory but, as will be witnessed by the photographs in this collection, times have changed significantly.

The *Berkshire* – now the *Reading* – *Chronicle* was founded in 1825 and has had a long history of reporting local news. Copies of the newspaper have survived, providing a reminder of more than 170 years of journalism in Reading. The decision to concentrate in this book on images of the period from the mid-1940s through to the early 1960s was based upon the survival of a large collection of high-quality glass negatives taken by the newspaper's photographers during those decades and now held by the Museum of Reading. These, along with the hand-written day books which give a description of each photograph taken, were deposited by the *Reading Chronicle* during the 1970s. Over the mid-century years photographs became more extensively used in the paper. Blocking images together on a single or double page was a standard practice at first, but gradually they were spread throughout the paper. Then in April 1956 the cover was changed from its traditional look of public notices, including deaths and marriages, to the type of headline news familiar today and front page photographs began to be used.

The decision to begin this book at the tail end of the Second World War was taken partially to avoid duplicating material published elsewhere, but also to start on a note of optimism. It was at this point that the people of Reading began re-establishing their lives for the future after the years of anxiety and hardship, moving forward into the optimistic 1950s, not to mention the vibrant 1960s. There were still social and economic battles to be won in the aftermath of war, but there was a sense of relief and determination to rebuild the spirit of the town. Sport, stage and cinema entertainment flourished, and many well-known personalities came to the town to the delight of the crowds.

The loss of old buildings and the construction of new changed the face of Reading forever. Sadly, elements of history were swept away in this progressive move, but a town with a modern eye on the future could not stand still.

A VE Day party in Eldon Street with a very well-laden table. Not only the children but soldiers home from the war were entertained to this feast.

CHAPTER ONE

A NEW BEGINNING

The journalist writing about the Reading Civil Defence Corps Display held at Hills Meadow gained an impression of changing times and receding memories of the war in 1960. He recalled: 'the heat of high summer tended to detract from the importance of the event and generally the crowd took the day lightly.' Yet the Civil Defence members worked hard to show their specialist skills with demonstrations including first aid and fire fighting. Certainly this air-to-air missile held no fear for the boys swarming over it.

In the autumn of 1943, as a car brought 23-year-old Frank Golder of Reading to Vachel Road, crowds surged to meet him. The car could go no further and Frank had to walk the rest of the way home on the wooden leg he had made for himself in a German prison camp. Neighbours mobbed him, patted him on the back and showered him with cigarettes. Flags hung from every house in the street, festooned from one side to the other, and above the door of no. 29 (his parents' house) was 'Welcome Home'. However, he and his wife were caught up in the problem which faced many young couples and families during and after the war – the lack of available housing. Finding themselves at the bottom of a long waiting list, they were forced to live with his parents.

Street parties were a popular and long-remembered part of the VE Day celebrations. Though the availability of food was heavily restricted, a special tea was provided for the children. Certainly here in Torrington Road, Whitley, everyone seemed to have joined in and enjoyed themselves.

Parades were a frequent and emotional sight immediately after the war, but between 1939 and 1945 parades and marches were particularly important to boost morale. In August 1941 a special 'Women's War Week' was held, which opened with a Sunday parade of women war workers (above). Crowds lined the streets to cheer the women in uniform and from factories who marched smartly side by side. 'The jolly girls from the Land Army supported by two farm tractors also won a loud cheer.'

On a memorable Sunday in May 1945 a victory parade was held through the centre of the town. The celebration of the end of the war with Germany was, as the Mayor said in his address, 'an historic occasion'. The procession was so long it took half an hour to pass the saluting base near the town hall. Those taking part 'showed a quiet and dignified beauty and were a credit to the organisations they represented'. Here the banners of Huntley Bourne & Stevens and Huntley & Palmers are seen passing from the Market Place to outside St Laurence's Church. The site of the People's Pantry, wrecked during the air raid in 1943, 'gave the energetic youth of the town a grandstand view of the march past'.

A major fire fighting rally was held in Reading in September 1943. This display of trick riding given by both men and women was one of many exciting events watched by a crowd of 3,000.

Sir Stafford Cripps, Minister of Aircraft Production, presented the awards at the Regional Finals of the Industrial Fire Services competition and gave an address to the firemen and firewomen taking part. Women were an important addition to the fire service during the war and it was this, among many other contributions, that would change their position in society in the postwar years.

When these air-raid shelters were delivered in pieces for assembly at Reading homes at the beginning of the war, no one knew how long they could last, and they added a gloomy aspect to streets and gardens. What a cheering contrast the photograph at the top of page 13 is!

Mr A.G. Reynolds of River Road, Reading, with his Anderson shelter nearing completion, March 1940. All it required was a covering of earth.

A speedy way of demolishing air-raid shelters in the streets of Reading, March 1946.

These tanks formed part of a parade through the town for National Thanksgiving Week. Admiral of the Fleet, Lord Chatfield, spoke at an assembly in the Forbury about the continued need for fund raising even in 1945. Money was desperately required in the struggle to return peace and prosperity to the country. Reading hoped to raise £1 million and was expected to achieve this high goal as it had achieved others during the war.

June 1945 saw a special afternoon of Victory in Europe celebrations in Palmer Park. The show started with a parade of decorated vehicles through Kings Meadow and on to the park. Another highlight was the children's fancy dress parade, and this knight on horseback was the clear winner. In his opening speech, the Mayor reminded everyone of the many sacrifices that had been made during the war and that there were still soldiers confronting the enemy in the Far East. One of these soldiers sent a message to the people of Reading for VE Day: 'Tell them to look after our old folk, our comrades and children, and say that the pleasures they display now are nothing to what will be shown when the job is finished and the victory finally achieved.'

During the summer of 1947 the Royal Engineers provided a demonstration for the public at Hills Meadow; it was carried out by a contingent from Aldershot. Large crowds watched the events including the main attraction, which was an 80 ft bailey bridge erected over the stream at the eastern end of Hills Meadow.

At the Battle of Britain Fête in 1949 the highlight was a grass-track racing display arranged, as the year before, by the South Reading Motor Cycle Club. A motor gymkhana, cycle polo match and even an egg and spoon race on two wheels gave great entertainment to the crowds.

'The magic of machinery': these boys appeared thoroughly absorbed when they inspected an aircraft engine at the ATC Information Bureau on Kings Road in 1942. The need to inspire and encourage cadets continued into the postwar years.

The Junior Military Tattoo at Christchurch Meadows in June 1962 was an event full of spectacle, with gliding by the Air Training Corps and a river crossing by the Sea Cadets. There was also a famous military figure present Field Marshal Lord Slim, one of the great soldiers of the Second World War. His advice to the 300 cadets at the tournament included always to 'own up and never to brag'.

The Battle of Britain Fête held at Dentons Field in September 1948 was one of a series of commemorations in Reading, which culminated in a service at St Mary's church. The programme of events included a fly-past and aerobatics demonstration by the RAF, and a motor cycle display by South Reading Motor Cycle Club. Here Air Vice-Marshal Williams can be seen chatting to the younger generation.

'Lunchtime shoppers and workers taking their midday stroll through the Forbury Gardens were surprised to see an unusual looking object mounted on an RAF trailer parked in the road. Some passed without stopping but others turned to investigate this curiosity which turned out to be one of the deadliest weapons produced by the Germans during the war. It was in fact the V1 Flying Bomb, perhaps more popularly known as the doodlebug. Its visit to Reading in January 1949 was part of a nationwide campaign to stimulate recruitment to the RAFVR as well as the Auxiliary Air Forces.' It was thought that by showing this weapon of modern war throughout the country, people could be made to realise that only by being prepared for a future conflict in which far more horrific weapons would undoubtedly be used, could such a war be avoided.

During Reading Thanksgiving Week in October 1945 many people visited the Thames Promenade near Caversham Bridge to see a German one-man submarine. She had been captured by the Royal Navy after being found adrift in the English Channel. She sank in Dover harbour but was raised in January 1945.

What might have been described as 'Operation Goering' was carried out in Minster Street in Reading in February 1951. The task was to get Hermann Goering's bullet-proof car into Messrs Heelas, where it was to be on exhibition. The 155 hp car was placed on its exhibition platform in just under twenty minutes by a detachment of soldiers from the MTDE of REME at Arborfield.

'Mass unemployment caused by fuel cuts, many Reading firms brought to a standstill.' On 10 February 1947 people found themselves plunged into what Mr Eden described as the nation's worst industrial crisis for twenty years. Here at Pulsometer Engineering Company initially only work not requiring electricity was undertaken. However, the problem was solved by installing diesel engines and a large percentage of the plant was brought back into operation.

Another important industry affected by the fuel crisis was Miles Aircraft at Woodley. Owing to government orders regarding electricity, machinery was forced to lie idle and workers found themselves without employment. Only those engaged in work using no fuel or electricity, such as these sheet metal workers, were able to carry on as normal.

Shopping at Boots the Chemist by candlelight during the fuel crisis of 1947.

The fuel shortage in 1947 created a demand for coal and here at Ayres depot residents are seen queuing for the meagre allowance.

One hundred people were forced to leave their homes after a 2,000 lb German Hermann bomb – a relic of the Second World War – was unearthed by a mechanical grab in gravel pits off Duffield Road in March 1961. The Ham River Company works foreman called in the bomb disposal squad of the Royal Engineers. One of the largest type of German bombs, measuring 5 ft in length and 2 ft in width, it was known to have been dropped on 9 June 1941. Here was some positive proof of the twenty-year-old legend of 'Foul-Weather Fritz', the German pilot who trained at Woodley and who flew for the Luftwaffe during the war. Rumour has it that because of his knowledge of the area, his superiors ordered him to lead raids on Woodley, but because he had so many friends there from pre-war years, he purposely missed every time. He was nicknamed 'Foul-Weather', because it was only then that he was able to miss the airfield without his colleagues becoming suspicious of his friendliness towards the people of Woodley.

In October 1951 the Rt Hon Aneurin Bevan spoke at a meeting held in support of Ian Mikardo and R.W.G. Mackay, Reading's Labour candidates for Parliament, at the Majestic Ballroom.

R.W.G. Mackay and Ian Mikardo seen with their agent Mr Grierson as they left the Town Hall after handing in their parliamentary nominations.

More than 300 people, mostly women, queued three deep for the chance to buy some nylon stockings in Broad Street in May 1949. Two adjacent shops announced that they would have stockings for sale from 10 a.m. and women began queuing at an early hour. First in the queue were two friends from Southampton Street who arrived at 5.45 a.m. Two Edinburgh men who arrived at 6.45 a.m. were near the front and were buying for their wives. One also wanted to send a pair of nylons to his daughter in Australia. Youngest in the queue, 13-year-old Alan Smith, of All Hallows Road, Caversham, wanted to get some for his mother. Supplies of fully fashioned stockings ran out after only forty minutes, while by 11.15 a.m. there were still long queues for seamless.

Opposite: Utilitarian, economical and streamlined – these appeared to be the first considerations when designing postwar electrical equipment for the home, judging by the All Electric Exhibition held in the small town hall in 1945. Featuring a number of labour-saving devices, the model kitchen on show was very impressive and highly desirable. No indication of cost and upkeep was given but the demonstrator assured potential customers that strong public demand would force down the prices. Individual electric units on show included a mixer-squeezer-potato-peeler machine, and a dish-washing device!

Acute housing shortages in the aftermath of the war forced some familes in the Reading area to become squatters in the summer of 1946. Occupation of huts at the old Army Ranikhet Camp at Tilehurst was rapid, with 200 people filling all the available space in just four days. The eighty families included an ex-sergeant instructor of the Royal Berkshire Regiment with his wife and two children who, hopeful that this was the end of their search for accommodation, named their hut 'Dun Roamin'. The local delivery men also took the opportunity to build up new custom (above).

'Not seen for a long time, eh?' A banana cutter at work in one of the ripening houses of O'Brien and Walkers at Reading. This was part of a consignment of bananas that came to the town early in 1946. Like oranges they had been virtually unobtainable during the wartime years.

CHAPTER TWO

THEY CAME TO READING

Tsai Chin attended a showing in the Town Hall of All These People *during the early summer of 1960 and afterwards took tea in the Mayor's Parlour. Here she discussed her West End success* The World of Suzi Wong *and the film which had given her the first major break in acting,* The Inn of the Sixth Happiness.

In April 1948 the Royal Standard flew alongside the Chinese Dragon of the Royal Berkshire Regiment at Brock Barracks. This was the first visit of King George VI since he had agreed to become the regiment's Colonel-in-Chief. Having driven to Brock Barracks through crowded and beflagged Reading streets, King George is seen here inspecting the regiment's war memorial.

Members of the Old Comrades Association were on parade for inspection and included many interesting individuals. Major G.H. Arbuthnot, eighty-three years of age, had joined the regiment in Egypt in 1885 and could remember being part of Queen Victoria's personal guard at Cowes in 1900.

Those visiting Reading during the war most frequently came with a specific purpose, as did the Duchess of Kent in January 1941. Her visit to see the work of the Women's Voluntary Services was greatly appreciated.

Princess Elizabeth paid a visit to Reading with her sister to see a performance given by Bertram Mills Circus in 1946. On arrival from Windsor, the princesses were received by the brothers Cyril and Bernard, sons of the circus's founder, who conducted them round the stables and menagerie. When they entered the Big Top, the audience immediately stood and they were presented with bouquets of roses.

During Reading's 'Wings for Victory Week' in June 1943 the Link Trainer, a popular feature of the RAF's exhibition at the Town Hall, held great interest for the Mayor Councillor W.E.C. McIlroy (seated) and Major Gwilym Lloyd George (standing behind him). The trainer was designed to teach a man to fly blind by instruments only. Major Lloyd George, the Minister for Fuel and Power had arrived in Reading in a car running on coke power – an economical novelty which it was hoped might catch on!

Dutch soldiers came to Reading's Vaudeville Cinema to see *Theirs is the Glory*, the epic story of the airborne troops of Arnhem. The operation was described as 'a daring venture that became the greatest drama ever told'. Remarkable in many ways, the film was not staged by actors but was made by the men who fought in the actual battle. On 17 September 1946 it was shown in London, Arnhem, Ottawa and in Reading.

During the autumn of 1960 the King of Nepal visited Berkshire and Reading. This was arranged by the Ministry of Agriculture who knew the King had a particular interest in British farming. Although the weather was typically English and umbrellas were the order of the day, King Mahendra seemed very impressed by the pedigree Hereford bull which he saw at the Cattle Breeding Centre and National Institute for Research in Dairying at Shinfield.

First-hand information of the 1953 Everest Expedition was given at Reading Town Hall in February 1954 by Mr T.D. Bourdillion and Mr C.W.F. Noyce. These two members of the expedition came to speak at a meeting arranged by Reading University Mountaineering Club, and students in particular packed the hall to hear them. Both paid high tribute to the splendid leadership of Col. Sir John Hunt. All proceeds from the talk went to the Everest Trust for the encouragement of research and exploration into the mountain ranges of the world.

Over 400 children heard Enid Blyton, the famous children's author, give a story hour at William McIlroy Ltd in Reading on a day in January 1953. It was her first provincial 'story hour' visit, following the success of similar occasions in large London stores. In her readings she introduced many of the hundreds of characters which she had created for children of all ages. Complete silence and rapt attention showed how the children appreciated her, as did the following two-hour signing session of her books. Her comment proved her own enjoyment of her visit: 'Reading children are absolutely delightful, most responsive and well behaved. They are among the best audiences I have ever had.'

Following in her ancestor's footsteps, Monica Dickens came to Reading in March 1955. However, rather than giving readings as Charles Dickens did in the Town Hall, she entertained enthusiastic young readers at W.H. Smiths in Broad Street by signing copies of her new book *Wings of Heaven*.

A qualified doctor, who had also brought laughter to thousands through the humour of his writing, gave Reading his full attention on an autumn day in 1955. This was Richard Gordon, well known for his bestseller *Doctor in the House*. He spent a hectic ninety minutes signing copies of his latest book, *Doctor at Large* and 207 copies were purchased on the spot.

The husband and wife team of Bernard Braden and Barbara Kelly were in Reading during June 1957 as part of a journey down the Thames, which was to be broadcast on the radio later in the summer. Though only a fragment of the river story could be told, they were introduced to some of its early history at Reading Museum and given a special reminder of their visit in the form of a flint axe head by the Director Mr W.A. Smallcombe.

Wilfred Pickles and his wife Mabel deserted radio and television for an evening in April 1957. The purpose of their visit to the Mitre Hotel was to join in with the 'Have a Go' competition on behalf of spastic children. An almost unbelievable 8 ft-high pile of pennies balanced on a pint mug raised £100, which Wilfred told customers would go towards their great aim of providing a holiday camp for the children.

Amid the weekend bustle of a busy Saturday at Reading station, the arrival of a VIP passed almost unnoticed by his fellow passengers. However the stationmaster, Mr J.F. Snow, was conscious of the necessary attention to be paid to the Home Secretary, R.A. Butler, when he came to a meeting in the town in November 1960.

Prior to the 1955 elections the Prime Minister, Sir Anthony Eden, came to Reading and spoke from the balcony of Somerset House opposite the Town Hall to a 3,000-strong crowd.

Douglas Bader's visit to Reading in April 1957 must have brought back poignant memories of the disastrous day in 1931 when his plane crashed at Woodley, resulting in the loss of both his legs. At least his return to the Royal Berkshire Hospital on this occasion was a pleasant experience; he came to present the prizes to the nurses at their annual prize-giving.

The climax of an evening's entertainment arranged by the Reading and District Association for Peace in June 1960 was the appearance of Paul Robeson. It was reported that this famous singer performed to one of the largest and most enthusiastic audiences seen in the Town Hall for a long time. It was also a memorable evening for the newly formed Reading Youth Choir, who had the thrill of joining with Paul Robeson and the Clarion Singers for a combined rendition of 'Jerusalem'. Neil Van Allen, the Canadian pianist (standing on the left), also took part in the concert.

Hundreds of excited fans besieged the tailoring shop owned by Mr A. Kogan at 60 Kings Road when his niece, the television, radio and recording star Alma Cogan came to open it officially for him. This visit to Reading in 1956 was a return to the place where she had spent her childhood, living in Broad Street, and where she remembered making her first stage appearance.

The guest of honour for the summer fête at Queen Anne's School, Caversham, in 1954 was the well-known actress Margaret Rutherford. As she stood looking at a stall the photographer managed to capture one of her famous facial expressions.

On a summer Saturday in 1962 the comedy star Hattie Jacques opened the annual fête at Battle Hospital for the League of Reading Hospitals. Described as an actress of 'comfortable dimensions' she immediately had the large crowd laughing. As she stepped on to the platform built for the opening ceremony, she began bouncing on it and called out to everyone: 'you know that's the only reason they got me along here today, to test this!' She volunteered to give her autograph for 6d a time and immediately there was a large demand.

The actor Richard Hearne, better known as Mr Pastry, toured Reading on a December morning in 1961 to raise money for the Berkshire Spastic Welfare Society and his own swimming pool scheme for spastics. He left the Town Hall in a highly decorated vintage car, travelled round the town and ended up at the Olympia for lunch. Here, in the afternoon, stalls and side shows continued to raise money; the total reached £850 by the end of the day. Students from the university had made themselves available to help him with collecting.

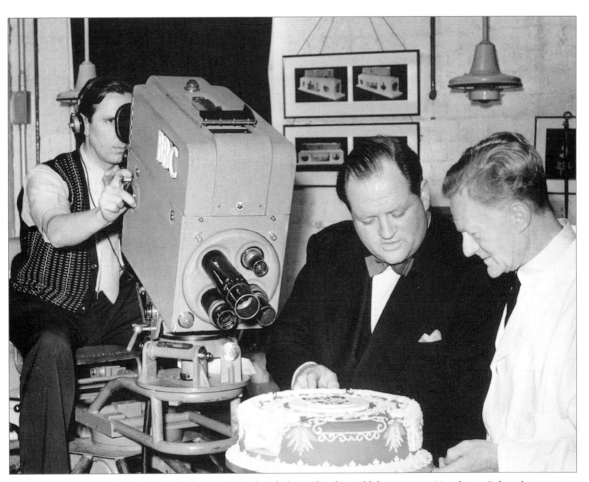

As part of Reading's week in the television limelight Richard Dimbleby came to Huntley & Palmer's to learn of the exciting skills used in icing sculpture. In the romantically named 'Bridal Cake Room' he watched Mr Jack Bryant put the finishing touches to a 20 lb cake for the Royal Berkshire Hospital. Animals such as rabbits, squirrels and even kangaroos were made in icing, each taking less than a minute to produce. During his working life of over forty years Mr Bryant decorated cakes for many members of the royal family, including the Queen and the Queen Mother.

In November 1958 the film star Richard Todd, who lived in the locality, came to Reading to open the annual bazaar of the Berkshire branch of the British Red Cross. Lady Benyon, holding the doll, and the Mayor of Reading, Councillor E.A. Busby, also supported this good cause. Autograph signing proved a very popular way of fund-raising — 1957's celebrity Robert Morley had raised over £1,000 (*see* p. 77). Hence the comment by Richard Todd: 'I hope the profits this year bear no relation to weight and age': he was a considerably lighter and more youthful actor!

CHAPTER THREE

THE CHANGING FACE
OF READING

In March 1962 the Palace, the last of Reading's professional live theatres, was reduced to a pile of rubble.
Such famous stars as Gracie Fields, Jack Buchanan and the cheeky Max Miller appeared at the theatre over
its fifty-five years of existence. It was opened in 1907 and had been designed to accommodate 1,600 people.
In its heyday every seat would have been taken and some would have stood to watch the performance, but
since 1960 the theatre had remained empty.

The shortage of housing for soldiers returning from the war and their families has already been mentioned as an acute problem. Many must have looked on with renewed hope and enthusiasm when they saw the first postwar building of houses by the Corporation at Whitley in April 1946. Prisoners of war were employed to dig trenches and lay mains.

Another method of assuring a house for one's family was to join a housing association. Here members of the Reading Housing Association can be seen in 1952, spending their Easter working on the foundations of houses that they were building for their own occupation at Caversham.

A new era for the town was heralded by modern buildings, including a new Reading Technical College. In October 1950 work began on the demolition of houses in Victoria Square to make way for the new college building.

The Birmingham sculptor, Mr William Bloye, put the finishing touches to the huge figure decorating the new Technical College in August 1954. 'George', as the figure was nicknamed, appeared to be holding a parchment while staring away to his right, and it was said to represent industry looking into the future.

'The Borough Surveyor is to be requested to arrange demolition of Finches Court, off Hosier Street, as soon as the remaining tenants have been rehoused.' So read the newspaper article in May 1959. These buildings were the remains of a mansion dating from the late sixteenth or early seventeenth century. Here, it is said, Lady Vachell, the daughter of Sir Francis Knollys, and her husband, the famous John Hampden, watched the Siege of Reading from the roof during the Civil War.

A view of the rear of Finches Buildings, situated near Hosier Street in the vicinity of St Mary's Butts, showing the character and architectural interest of these dwellings. Incorporated in the north wall were squared stones reused from the site of the dissolved Reading Abbey. However, serious dilapidation and the demands of postwar town redevelopment were to put the future of these buildings in jeopardy.

A sad sight in November 1960. A heap of debris was all that remained of one of the oldest houses in Reading, Finches Buildings. 'With their demolition goes not a little of the town's history.'

A few strokes from this modern version of the battering ram, and down came one of the oldest buildings at Huntley & Palmers. The buildings demolished in November 1962 were those formerly devoted to wafer production; they had been empty since the company had moved this area of biscuit making to its factory in Liverpool.

Blagrave Cottages, situated behind Blagrave Buildings in Friar Street on the north side shortly before Grey Friars Road, were described in the 1860s as 'model lodging houses'. They were part of the 'Blagrave Property' in the town and had been built at the sole expense of J.H. Blagrave of Calcot Park. However, by 1961 they were condemned as unfit for human habitation and were scheduled for demolition.

Blagrave Buildings were a substantial group of flats or tenements with shops beneath in Friar Street, and though they survived a little longer than Blagrave Cottages they suffered the same fate in 1962 and were demolished to make way for part of modern Reading.

High above the roar of Reading's traffic in September 1955 workmen demolished 16 Friar Street, the ivy-clad building and well-known landmark in the centre of the town.

Another piece of Reading disappeared in November 1960. This time it was the demolition of Abbey Brook Cottages adjoining Soundys Mill in Abbey Square, to make way for a County Council car park.

In August 1959 the journalist who wrote this article put forward his feelings in dashing prose. 'This is the age of noise; nerve-racking noise both on the ground and in the air. Our towns and cities have become a Dante-esque drama, growing in intensity as the days pass. One of the main highways of Reading is "up". The old tramlines in Caversham Road are being removed and the road surface renewed. Traffic is being diverted smoothly but the scene is reminiscent of the unhappy days when, under enemy action, such upheavals were commonplace. Pneumatic drills stutter the day long, piercing the road and the eardrums, a staccato inferno in the dust-laden air. It is all very perturbing, especially for those living in the vicinity; but it clearly has become necessary and is the price we pay for what is called progress.'

A small but highly efficient piece of digging equipment is caught by the camera ripping up the old tramlines with ease, and on this summer day in 1950 it obviously provided good entertainment for all the men and boys in the neighbourhood.

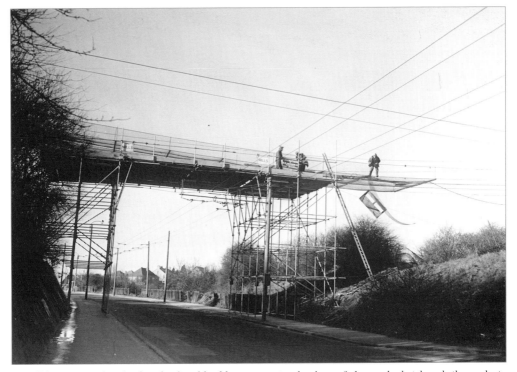

A well-known Reading landmark, the old cableway carrying buckets of clay to the brick and tile works in Water Road, was dismantled in February 1960 to make way for more modern methods of transporting clay. This work is taking place on the stretch over Norcot Road in Tilehurst.

Platform 4 at Reading General station was never to be the same again after being part of the £2¼ million modernization scheme undertaken in March 1961. This picture shows the work in progress, strengthening the subway roof to make way for a new platform and down line. Naturally all had to be done in stages to ensure that the normal running of the station could continue. Nevertheless swinging this huge girder into place was apparently quite a task to be finished in time for the Monday rush-hour.

'Topping out', an ancient custom of the building trade, was observed in January 1960 when Leslie and Company Ltd, building contractors of London and Darlington, hoisted the Union Jack and their own flag on the roof of the new building they were erecting for the Prudential Assurance Company at 21–23 Valpy Street. All the men working on the site stopped to have a pint of beer on the firm. Tradition has it that if no free drinks were provided, the Union Jack would be replaced by a black flag to denote a curse.

A view from Reading's giant gasholder, erected in the 1930s, into the first section of its 'twin', which was in the course of construction in 1955. Beyond the framework Sutton Seeds' trial grounds were flourishing, while to the right lay the Southern Railway line.

Demolition proposals for 22 The Forbury prompted an outraged letter of protest to the *Chronicle* in September 1961. The plans for the new ring road would result in the loss 'of one of the few buildings left in the town of outstanding beauty and architectural merit and of historic interest. Can nothing be done to save this and other such buildings by an upsurge of indignation and protest from the people of Reading? Or must everything give way before the giant motor-car?' Parliamentary approval had been granted for its demolition, though it was hoped that efforts would be made to save important removable features such as the staircase. Preservation of the building at that time could only have been achieved by the Corporation revoking the planning consent that it had already given, 'a rare and unlikely course of action'. The building was demolished soon afterwards.

CHAPTER FOUR

NATIONAL NEWS

Reading celebrated the coronation of Queen Elizabeth II in a number of ways, not least the magnificent decorations put up on buildings throughout the town. All the major businesses contributed by decorating their own premises, and various public buildings, such as the Town Hall, joined in the festivities.

The Town Hall coronation decoration in the course of preparation, 1953.

The main entrance to Reading station decorated for the coronation.

H. & G. Simonds, the brewers, managed to use the bridge between two of their buildings in Bridge Street as part of the decorative scheme.

The large 1930s façade of the entrance and offices for Huntley & Palmers gave great scope for an eye-catching design.

Standing out above the stall in the Market Place, Sutton & Sons added further colour and spectacle to their already elaborate Victorian building.

Suttons also decorated their attractive entrance adjacent to the Forbury Gardens. In the distance the Abbey Gateway can be seen and on the far right is the corner of 22 The Forbury, a gracious building that was to suffer the fate of demolition within a few years of this date (*see* p. 54).

Heelas chose an elaborate crown as the centrepiece of their coronation decoration.

Miles Aircraft at Woodley quickly became involved in civil aviation development in postwar years, having also substantially contributed to aviation during the war. People in the Reading district may well have noticed an unusually shaped aircraft in the sky at this time, the early part of summer 1945. This was the new Miles Aerovan, which when demonstrated to a group of newspaper journalists was compared with travelling on a luxury bus. With a cruising speed of 110–15 mph it was equally suitable for carrying freight or passengers, and was amusingly described as 'the taxi-cab or delivery van of the future'.

By 1954, when this picture was taken, Handley Page Reading Ltd had taken over the production departments of the aviation industry at Woodley. At the aerodrome international rather than national news was made when Sir Frederick Handley Page formally handed over the first of two Marathon airliners for service with Far Eastern Airlines. Todomu Nakamura, aviation manager for the company's agents in Japan, received the certificate of airworthiness.

In March 1962 Reading found itself one of a total of forty-five sites named as part of a national 'Panda' experiment. It was hoped that the introduction of the push-button control unit would be a modern advance on the old type of zebra crossing. It was given an experimental period of twelve months, after which the Minister of Transport was to review effects on the pedestrian and the driver.

In December 1962 an exceptional boring operation took place in Reading organized by the Southern Gas Board. Two 382 ft lengths of steel tube with an 18 in diameter were laid to create a pipeline some 30 ft below the main railway line through the town. Believed to be the largest 'thrust-bore' operation at the time in the country, it surpassed in size the one at Hyde Park Corner, London, which was connected with the underpass there.

Two men arrived in Reading on a cold January day in 1956 after spending a week paddling their canoe down the Kennet & Avon Canal from Bath. Their plan was to hand a petition to the Queen in protest at the threatened closure of the canal, and they had collected nearly 21,000 signatures. Over 100 people turned out at High Bridge to welcome Lt Cdr C. Wray-Bliss and Cdr J. Sheldon, and to hear of the hazards of their journey.

When the Ministry of Works Building Plant Exhibition was held in Reading in June 1954, the site at Hills Meadow at last came into its own. The exhibition organizers regarded it as the 'finest and best situated showground' ever placed at their disposal. Covering a 10-acre site with sixty exhibitors, mostly British, the exhibition was the seventh and largest of its kind. Any worries over flooding were overcome with the help of Thames Conservancy, who made adjustments at Caversham and Sonning Lock to lower the water level of the Thames. After major London exhibitions this was seen as an opportunity to bring such a show out of the capital and to the people. 'It is an amazing exhibition for which the public as a whole should be delighted to pay their "bobs" for admission.'

'Never before can Reading have seen anything quite like this protest march.' This was the comment reported on more than 1,000 'Ban the Bomb' protestors who arrived in St Mary's Butts on Good Friday 1958, weary from their march which had commenced in Trafalgar Square.

During the 1958 March the protesters stayed in Reading over the weekend where they were given sleeping accommodation mainly in local schools, though some private homes offered hospitality. Then on the Monday they pressed on along the Bath Road, beside the newly built block of flats, to walk the eight miles to the Atomic Weapons Research Establishment at Aldermaston.

Easter weekend 1960 saw the largest anti-nuclear weapons march up to this date pass through Reading. The 3,000 marchers of the previous year had not just doubled as was expected but were 10,000 strong. Some participants were certainly of a tender age!

The first gas turbine engine ever to be used for passenger service stopped at Reading Western station in May 1950; it was on the normal passenger service from Paddington to Cheltenham. The driver was strongly in favour of the new engine, seeing it as a great improvement over the steam engine and much easier to handle. No longer would he have to contend with fire and steam, but could operate the controls in a clean cab. The engine was made in Switzerland.

CHAPTER FIVE

ENTERTAINMENT

The well-known actor Donald Sinden came with his wife to Reading in December 1959 to join in the celebration for the reopening of the Odeon cinema after a major refurbishment, which transformed Reading's largest cinema into one that could rate itself alongside those in the West End of London. Here Roy Green, the doorman, and the usherettes modelling their new uniforms were caught enjoying a joke with the star, whose many film performances included the 'Doctor' series and The Cruel Sea.

During Donald Sinden's visit to Reading he spent the afternoon at the Huntley & Palmers factory, where all the girls were anxious to catch a glimpse of him. To their surprise and delight he made a point of talking and joking with them, and was happy to sign photographs. He also took great interest in the biscuit making!

Another film star who made a personal appearance when her film was showing in Reading was Valerie Hobson. Early in 1950 the new John Mills production came to the Odeon, *The Rocking Horse Winner*, adapted from a short story by D.H. Lawrence.

'Machine gun fire and the desultory sound of small arms rocked the peace of Reading's town centre on Monday evening.' This was the opening of an interesting story on some highly original publicity organized by the manager of the Odeon cinema to promote the film *The Guns of Navarone*. This epic story told of the destruction of two major radar-controlled German guns on the Greek island of Navarone. So on an October day in 1961 the SAS gallantly re-enacted a number of shots from the film. They stormed a 'radar station' on the roof of the cinema and abseiled at great speed down the sheer face of the building.

Jack Warner, the film and radio star, joined members of the WVS to entertain a gathering of the Darby and Joan Club at Palmer Park on an autumn day in 1951.

Winifred Attwell came to Reading on a cold January day in 1958 not only to entertain the town but to use Reading Town Hall to record her show for Radio Luxembourg. Packed audiences sat enthralled to hear her two recordings which were programmed to go on air in March. She naturally featured her two pianos, one grand and the famous 'other', as seen here with the husband and wife singing team of Pearl Carr and Teddy Johnson. Her show was voted the top music show on Radio Luxembourg in 1957.

The 'Miss Reading' competition was once an annual highlight on the town's calendar. Pictures of the attractive young entries were shown in the paper for some weeks before and there was full coverage of the always interesting line-up of judges. The chosen Miss Reading of 1957, Rosemary Brown, found herself with some competition for the limelight from a very popular judge, the actor Terry-Thomas. Appearing in an exotic waistcoat, with cigarette holder and red carnation, he received a terrific welcome, and spoke to the audience for ten minutes.

In the finals of the 'Ideal Barmaid' competition held at the Central cinema in April 1960, Margaret Donaghy of the White Hart Hotel was chosen as the prize winner. It was not only her appearance and personality that caught the eyes of the judges, but her ability to pour a glass of ale from a bottle showed that this is an art in itself. The ladies, left to right: Margaret Donaghy, Miss Anita Gould, Miss Daphne Benjamin, Mrs Iris Potter.

The newly formed drama group at Battle Secondary School found themselves performing to an expert in the field when the film star Alec Guinness visited to see their current production in March 1953. The play was *Lady Precious Stream*, an ancient Chinese drama. Alec Guinness had a connection with the school through the then headmaster, Mr L. Davidson, who had taught him in the past and had given him his first acting part.

Entertainment in the making in September 1951, when a film crew and stars came to Reading to make a film from the book by Arnold Bennett, *The Card*. In casual poise, the actors, Alec Guinness, Veronica Turleigh and Petula Clark were caught going through the script of a scene with the director Ronald Neame.

A sequence from *The Card* is filmed outside the Milk Marketing Board's office in Christchurch Road.

In December 1961 the well-known actress from a famous theatrical family, Vanessa Redgrave, joined the Progress Theatre in celebrating its past successes. An exhibition of photographs of many of their productions must have brought back intriguing memories to all those involved, and Miss Redgrave seemed to take an appreciative view of this with Norman Bishop.

'Yet another Mikado' was the comment by the paper; 'why do they choose it?' The reply was that Gilbert and Sullivan could not help but draw the public. This production, by the Sainsbury Singers in 1956, was certainly a magnificent spectacle, and the newspaper review was full of compliments.

A perfect venue for outdoor entertainment: three members of the Berkshire Shakespeare players are holding a rehearsal for their production of James Birdie's *Tobias and the Angel* at Caversham Court in June 1960.

Instruction through entertainment was the message from Coco the Clown, but he did consider his work a serious matter. In March 1963 Coco started two days of visits to Reading schools to give his popular road safety talks to children. He commented that when lecturing at schools, cinemas or clubs he had a better response when dressed in his clown outfit. Traffic and busy roads made this work all the more important, particularly in town-centre schools. E.P. Collier School in York Road was lucky to be on his visiting list.

Two elephants that heralded the arrival of the circus in town certainly attracted the children. After the war years, with restrictions on all pleasures and luxuries, the appearance of the circus in the summer of 1949 was a happy reminder that life was gradually getting back to normal.

Robert Morley, the actor-manager, opened the autumn bazaar of the Berkshire Branch of the Red Cross in 1957 at the Town Hall. He seemed to thoroughly enjoy his shopping spree, attended by some of the junior members.

More topical entertainment, in the form of the 'King and Queen of Twist', took place at the Majestic Ballroom in March 1962, sponsored by the *Reading and Berkshire Chronicle*. Second place out of twenty contestants was given to these very agile dancers Laura Darling and David Gask.

Bongo drum fever hit Reading with the arrival of the film *Expresso Bongo* at the Central and the Granby in February 1960. Starring Lawrence Harvey, Cliff Richard and Sylvia Sims, it was tipped by many experts to be one of the box office winners for the year. To complement the film, an Expresso Bongo Dance was held at the Olympia Ballroom, and to add to the fun the management of the Central cinema arranged a bongo drumming competition. The star drummer turned out to be a visitor from Oxford, Tony Wirdnam, who won the first prize – a set of bongo drums!

A new national craze for bingo hit Reading in 1961 and the opening session of the Premier Bingo Club at Reading Town Hall was well reported in the newspapers. Four hundred and fifty people attended on that first evening, and although it was not to start until 8.15 p.m. queues of enthusiastic players were outside by 6.15 p.m.

Everyone seemed to be concentrating hard but at the same time thoroughly enjoying themselves at the first session of bingo to be held at the Town Hall. Apparently there was good-natured banter when the lucky ones shouted 'House'.

'The Little Man's Dog Show' was another event filmed by the BBC during its spotlight on Reading week in July 1954. Staged at the Jack of Both Sides public house, it was organized on the lines of those held in the Midlands and the North of England, where dogs of different breeds met each other in a knock-out competition. Here Mr Alf Rose of Barnetby, Lincolnshire, was demonstrating a racing start with his whippet 'Penny'.

Reading's television week profile in 1954 came to a close with an afternoon programme from the Thameside Promenade at Caversham. Everyone seemed to want to join in the fun and the river was so crowded with small boats that there was hardly room for them all; hundreds of spectators also turned up.

Hywel Davies, commentator for the BBC, paid many compliments to the variety of craft on the river and could not have failed to comment on this splendid camping skiff, which showed the truly relaxing way to holiday on the Thames. However, when the cameras stopped turning the armada of boats and the great crowds suddenly disappeared.

Reading was treated twice over in March 1945, for not only was the excellent film *It's Hard to Be Good* showing at the Vaudeville, but the star of the film, Jimmy Handley, also paid a visit to the town. In his part as a young army officer, thought to be one of his best to that date, he found out the hard way that it is not possible to put the world to rights single-handed. It was described as 'a very good unpretentious comedy'. The star still found plenty of time to meet the people of Reading and to sign autographs.

CHAPTER SIX

SPORT

Former World Champion motor-cyclist John Surtees, who at this time in 1961 was making a name for himself on four wheels, was seen giving encouragement to competitors at the start of the Road Courtesy Rally for motor-cyclists which set off from Hills Meadow.

Ardent supporters were prepared to queue to make sure of getting their tickets for the third round cup tie between Reading and Swansea in January 1952. On the day, although Reading had all the play and victory over Swansea was expected, it was Swansea who got the three goals.

In November 1960 Reading's win against Kettering put them into the third round of the FA Cup to face Barnsley. A crowd of 12,500 supporters watched this match at Elm Park, where Bill Lacy provided the scoring power for this 4–2 victory.

Before the match in February 1958 between Reading and Crystal Palace, the players and officials lined up, and after a band had played a verse of 'Abide with me' they stood in silence with the crowd, remembering the Manchester players who had lost their lives in the recent air disaster in Munich. One of the Crystal Palace players, David Berry, was the younger brother of John Berry, a Manchester player who was seriously injured in the crash. Matt Busby, the Manager of Manchester United, with the late Frank Swift, had entertained the Reading crowds at Elm Park during the war years with their 'football artistry'.

A special football match played in the spring of 1959 turned out to be a 'day to remember'. It was the All Star XI *v* Huntley & Palmers at Palmer Park, and the stars included Ronnie Corbett, Tommy Steele, Jess Conrad, Lonnie Donegan, Alfie Bass and Mike and Bernie Winters. This charity match, as one can imagine, turned into a riotous event and the compères Paul Carpenter and June Cunningham found it impossible to keep the score!

Ronnie Corbett got his 'marching orders' at the All Stars' charity match at Palmer Park, but it seems unlikely that he stayed off the pitch for very long!

With the Big Freeze still persisting in February 1963, Reading's footballers themselves clearing the snow at Elm Park.

An exhibition golf match was played in Reading with the partnership of Charlie Drake and Ben Warriss against two professionals, Pat Roberts (Reading) and Roy Mason (Goring and Streatley). This was part of a gala weekend held by Reading Golf Club to celebrate its jubilee in 1960. The professionals, as expected, were the winner, but on occasions were surpassed by the excellent driving of the left-hander Ben Warris, and Charlie Drake proved to be a 'wizard' on the green.

Surrey and England cricketer Ken Barrington, who was born and went to school in Reading, tried his hand at a hoop-la stall accompanied by his wife and Alderman George Holley, after he had opened the Mount Pleasant Youth Club bazaar in 1959.

Peter May, England's cricket captain, returned to his home town of Reading in 1956 to sign copies of his new book. He also signed bats, autograph albums and photographs, and even 'scruffy little bits of paper proffered by shy hero-worshipping youngsters'. This was his last visit before he departed on an African tour and one five-year-old gave him the parting good wish: 'I hope you score hundreds'!

In September 1956 the British Motor Cycle Team, who were about to leave for Germany, met a BBC television cameraman from *Sportsview* at Stocker and Shepherd Ltd, motor cycle agents in the Oxford Road. The team was studying routes for a six-day trial at Garmisch-Partenkirchen.

Stock-car racing began at Reading Stadium in June 1962 before a capacity audience of 10,000 and with 100 drivers, which was the largest number recorded at a meeting in Britain. It was the town's first taste of another 'big time' sport. Split Waterman, former speedway ace, officially opened the new track at Reading Greyhound Stadium; it was reckoned to be one of the fastest in the country.

In May 1962 the *Chronicle* Gala Night
of Sport took place at Palmer Park,
and one of the main attractions for
the 4,500 fans was Yorkshire's Derek
Ibbotson running in the mile race.
The odds seemed against a fast time as
he had been at an exhibition in
London all day before driving the 39
miles to Reading, and the track itself
was already damaged by previous
events. However, to the thrill of the
crowd he produced the fastest mile
yet run that year.

Mary Bignal and her Olympic
oarsman husband Sydney Rand
were spotted at Palmer Park
talking with Berkshire
International runner Stan Eldon
during May 1961. At this time
they were living in Henley and
came over to Reading for three or
four evenings each week to put in
training sessions at the track.

Reading Amateur Regatta in June 1961 was a most successful event for Reading Rowing Club, beating Reading University to take the Maiden Erlegh Cup for junior-senior fours.

A July day in 1961 proved to be a nightmare as far as the Working Men's Regatta in Reading was concerned. Held in Dreadnought Reach, it was recorded that the oarsmen faced 'a mile of misery' on this normally placid part of the Thames. On land it was hardly better, where officials and spectators fought to save marquees being uprooted by a violent storm. In a quieter moment, however, the opportunity for free rowing coaching was eagerly taken up by keen youngsters.

Glorious sunshine came to Reading on the day of the Regatta in 1957, which was most encouraging as more often than not the event was marred by a downpour of rain. Prizes were presented by Sir Eric Harrison, High Commissioner for Australia.

The 1957 Reading Regatta was broadcast by the BBC with top commentators Raymond Glendenning (left) and John Snagge (right). One of those interviewed was the Olympic silver medallist Stuart A. Mackenzie, from Sydney, Australia, who was the winner of the Senior Sculls.

CHAPTER SEVEN

UNUSUAL DAYS

*Shrove Tuesday was not to be forgotten in 1960 by the students of
Reading Technical College, who had a true pancake day fling!*

A rather different family pet followed Mrs Rogers on her shopping expedition in Tilehurst during mid-summer in 1949. Neither of them looks perturbed by this outing, but one wonders whether some of the other shoppers might have found it a little surprising.

Possibly Reading's oldest angler, Mr Edward Theobald, was caught on this day in October 1958 setting out on his motor cycle for the Thames. Although 'Ye Olde Thames Anglers' Club' tried to encourage younger members to join, they were pleased to boast that their oldest member was eighty-six years of age. It was rumoured that he used to climb out of a back window of his house when a boy, without his parents knowing, and go fishing from 2.30 a.m. until it was time for school!

The ATV presenter Miss Penny Knowles seemed determined to give Reading an unusual day when she appeared in Blagrave Street riding a camel in the middle of November 1955. For her programme *Penny to See a Peep-Show*, she was always trying to feature stories which were out of the ordinary, and Reading proved to be the largest nearby town to parade one of the camels from Bertram Mills Circus at Ascot.

Something out of the ordinary happened in Caversham in July 1950, when a group of ten steers broke loose in the Gosbrook Road area. They were only captured after a chase lasting two hours.

The police gave chase to some of the escaped cattle in George Street while the local children ran for safety. The steers were finally caught in Sutton & Sons' yard in the Forbury.

Why was Reading chosen in 1961 as the town in which the revolutionary 'Daily Dial' free telephone information service made its world debut? It turned out that Mr J. Marshall, the Managing Director of the Provincial Recording Co. Ltd, which was to operate the service, lived at Langley Hill in Tilehurst. So John Tidmarsh of the BBC programme *Town and Around* came to interview Mr Marshall and to record the first trial calls of the service.

It was a strange day for Reading when it was described as 'a very dirty town' by two local government officers visiting from British Commonwealth countries. Mr Grannum, the Town Clerk of Bridgetown in Barbados, admitted that there were no big industrial towns in his country, but he could not imagine where all the dirt came from. These comments came as a surprise to listening journalists who thought that Reading was known as a clean town.

In November 1953 the Regal cinema in Caversham not only had an exceptional film showing but was privileged to have a special guest to attend one of the performances. The newly released film *Titanic* was the epic story of the tragedy and Mr J. Coles, the manager of the Regal, had invited Mr E.C. Judd of 18 Westfield Road, who was himself a surviving member of the crew.

One would naturally expect to have found a stagedoor keeper at the Palace Theatre, in 1959, but 'Old Harry,' as Mr Harry Baverstock of Cardiff Road was known, was rather unusual, still working at eighty-nine years of age. Even Diana Dors was known to have had to wait at the stagedoor while 'Old Harry' checked with the management that she could come in. He had taken up his position when he had retired from being storeman of the Trade Union Club in Minster Street, and commented: 'If I gave up work I would die.'

This is not something one might expect to see every day, a 'Thread the Needle Race' – for the Reverend Fathers and the Reverend Brothers at the St Joseph's Convent sports. It is not as easy as it looks! Even during the war in 1944 there were still moments in life to be light-hearted.

The giant hull of a boat being taken to the west of England by road in 1951 gave some problems as it passed through Reading. This photograph, taken at Cemetery Junction, gives an idea of its size.

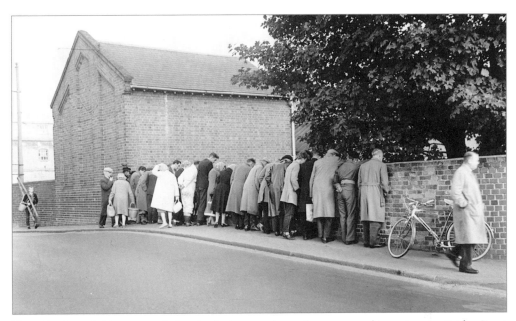

These Reading inhabitants provoked an intriguing question as they were caught peering over Bridge Street bridge on an autumn day in 1961. They were in fact looking at a police frogman searching for jewellery that was thought to have been thrown into the Kennet.

It was an important day for all those interested in the future of the Kennet & Avon Canal when the NB *Enterprise* made her maiden voyage on a passenger service between Reading and Burghfield. The television cameras were present to record this fifty-year-old converted narrow barge take its first group of passengers, which included Ann Morse, Miss Reading 1958, and Lord Methuen, the President of the K & A Canal Association. In 1956 the British Transport Commission had tried to close the canal but had been refused permission by Parliament. On this day in March 1958 the prospects for its future looked more encouraging.

Twenty-one of the district nurses employed by Berkshire County Council had the pleasure of swapping their old Morris Minors for brand new Mini-Minors early in 1960. They are pictured here at Hewin's Garage, Castle Street. A telling comment came from one nurse, 'no more cold feet'; they were delighted to here that the cars were equipped with heaters.

These Austin Healey Sprites, described as 'those diminutive goggle-eyed sports cars' were always of interest on the Reading roads and were rallied together at the Three Tuns for the inaugural meeting of a local section of the Sprite Owners Club in January 1960.

Certainly it was a special day for the children's ward of the Royal Berkshire Hospital when a huge cake appeared in the shape of a car. This was presented by Hewin's of Reading to celebrate the production of the millionth Morris Minor.

Two giant cheeses from the Scottish Milk Marketing Board were definitely an unusual sight in the centre of Reading. These 'jumbos' were some of the largest cheeses in the world, each weighing over ½ ton, they were on their way to the dairy show in London. In October 1957 Reading was their last port of call on their 700-mile journey, and the Mayor found himself presented with a 'normal' sized 40 lb Dunlop cheese.

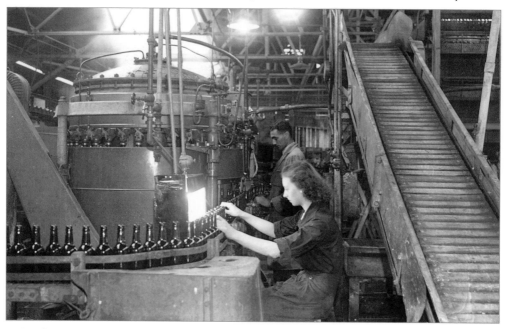

In October 1947 Messrs H. & G. Simonds prepared a special beer to be bottled and presented to HRH Princess Elizabeth and Lt Phillip Mountbatten on the occasion of their wedding.

An unusual baker, Mr E.F. 'Teddy' Tong of Earley believed himself to be the only muffin and crumpet maker of any consequence in the country in 1961. As a boy he learnt the art of crumpet making from an old man helping him at 4 a.m. After the First World War he set up his own bakery business, and originally travelled round Earley with a basket of muffins and a bell. With the help of his wife and son (seen here with Mr Tong) the business had successfully prospered.

In 1953 students took the request to keep Reading clean after Rag Week quite literally, and scrubbed down a pedestrian crossing after the procession had passed.

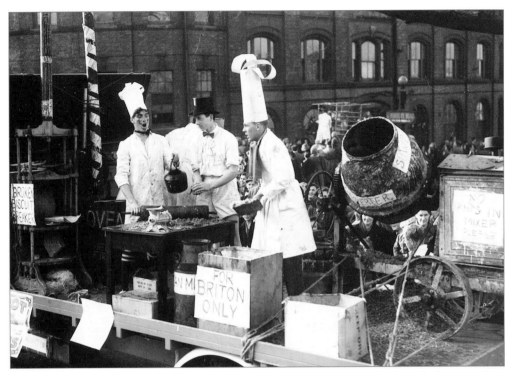

It appears that cleanliness had slipped a little in previous years if one looks closely at the biscuit-making float for the rag procession in 1952.

These Reading students found themselves roped in by their girlfriends to knit a scarf, to help break the world record length of 280 ft which at that time was held by a Canadian University. It was one of the unusual stunts for Rag Week in 1963.

A student fortune-teller captivated a young crowd in Reading Market Place in 1948.

An unusual beast found his way into the sale ring at Reading's famous Cattle Market during Rag Week in 1948.

Screaming Lord Sutch, a cult figure of the more extreme 1960s, came to excite and entertain the younger generation in Reading. Performing at the Majestic Ballroom, his graveyard scene entrance from a coffin amidst smoke and green lighting effects was certainly dramatic. With 18-inch long hair, and his customary top hat, he apparently claimed his success was due to his 'originality'.

Who in 1955 could claim to be Reading's oldest full-time worker? Certainly there would be few to challenge 'Snowie Rush'. At eighty-four years of age he was still working a 45-hour week as a brick-layer, and his work at that time was putting the finishing touches to a tall chimney 60 ft above the ground, part of the old people's home at Parkhurst on the Bath Road. He had enlisted in 1888, fought in the Battle of Omdurman in 1889 and spent four years fighting in the First World War. His own comment in 1955 was: 'I've worked on some of the highest buildings in Reading, and I see no reason why I should give up now.'

CHAPTER EIGHT

TO THE RESCUE

There was excitement for a Monday morning crowd in Station Road when a fireman on a turntable ladder high above removed a chimney pot loosened by gale-force winds. This followed an incident a short while earlier when an elderly man was injured by part of a chimney-stack which had fallen from the Pearl Insurance buildings. High winds brought havoc to many parts of Reading on that February day in 1961.

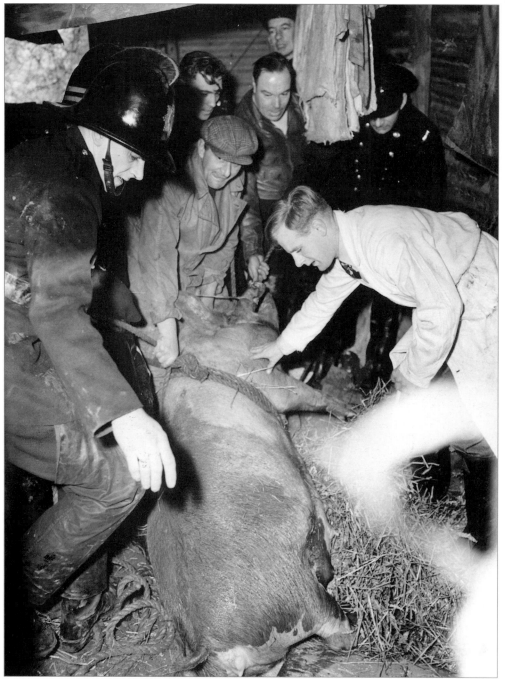

A pig with a story to tell appeared in the Reading news in February 1957. Leaving the safety of her shed in Scours Lane, Tilehurst, she fell head first down an 8 ft deep well. Naturally she became stuck, and a full-scale rescue operation from the fire brigade was required. Eight men hauled all 600 lb of her out of the well. The sow was unharmed apart from a few scratches, and was led away for a happy event – the delivery of a litter of piglets.

A champion Clydesdale, three times winner at the Wokingham Agricultural Show was rescued by firemen and farm workers after he had become trapped in a 6 ft ditch at Worton Grange in 1959. Eleven-year-old 'Prince', who weighed over a ton, was thought to have floundered for some time and sunk more deeply into the mud. The Berkshire and Reading Fire Brigade spent more than an hour using a sling to free him.

'A night of terror' was experienced by residents in the Bryanston Square area of the Oxford Road. The September night in 1946 saw one of the most disastrous fires in Reading for many years. With 50-ft flames roaring beside them, women and children queued calmly for their turn to run to safety through the one pathway of escape from the Square. A sawmill belonging to Warwick Bros Ltd, timber merchants, and four houses were completely destroyed, with the cost of the damage in excess of £50,000. The fire was thought to have started in the sawmill.

A dramatic picture of a railway engine derailed at Southcote Junction in June 1949.

This wreckage was caused by the collision between three goods wagons and a parcel train outside Reading General station in September 1957. Fortunately the wagons were not loaded and were stationary on a loop line when the accident happened; no one was hurt.

A furniture van met with a mishap on an April day in 1949, and completely blocked Grove Hill in Caversham.

The ultimate nightmare when moving! The only way to bring the removal van upright on Grove Hill was to unload all the customer's furniture.

A tanker containing sugar provided Reading with a rather unusual accident in 1960. Before moving the tanker it was felt that the sugar should be removed and the only possible way was for someone to get inside and shovel it out into sacks: hardly an easy job! The comment made by the newspaper at the time was: 'we wonder if he likes sugar in his tea?'

A near disastrous accident by the River Kennet in the centre of Reading happened on a summer day in 1954. A young angler reported his memory of the occasion: 'I threw in my line and then a motor lorry landed on the bank beside me!'

A London woman may have regretted coming to Reading in August 1958 after her alarming experience with her saloon car at Cemetery junction. First she collided with the back of a car being driven by her husband. Then her car shot across the road and collided with a motor coach before coming to rest an the green verge of the roundabout. The car was badly damaged and had four burst tyres, but fortunately no one appeared to have been hurt.

The rapid thaw in March 1947, following the severe weather of the winter, produced the worst floods experienced in the lives of most people in the Thames Valley. Many people were forced to live in the upstairs rooms of their houses as the ground floor was completely flooded. Boats were the only means of transport, though even reaching the boat was far from easy!

Tradesmen found that the only way to make their rounds during the 1947 floods was by boat, as here in Washington Road, Caversham.

A desolate scene in Great Knollys Street where the road appeared more like a river during the floods of 1947.

Near Caversham Bridge, the course of the river, as in many places, completely disappeared in 1947. Its overall height was several feet above that normally known, though not quite as high as it had been in 1894.

Workmen at Caversham weir in 1947 fought a battle to keep the sluice gates clear of obstacles, including parts of trees blown down by the gales and then carried down river by the swollen waters.

Not needing rescuing but experiencing a noticeable heatwave in 1949, these Reading men and women were out enjoying their lunch-hour in the Forbury Gardens.

One might have thought that Reading had battle with enough water problems in 1947, but one has to admit that this water spout in St Mary's Butts caused by a burst water main was rather spectacular and probably quite cooling on a hot summer's day in July.

Heavy snow hit Southern England on Boxing Day 1962, and by January 1963 the conditions were already being described as 'the worst in living memory'. Keeping the roads open throughout the county was a great problem and essential milk, vegetables, paraffin and coal were rapidly reduced to short supply. These children took advantage of the 'Big Freeze' to enjoy the snow and ice down at Christchurch Meadows.

Prospect Park became an ideal place to practise skiing after the heavy snows of 1963.

ACKNOWLEDGEMENTS

I should like to thank Karen Hull, Javier Pes, Steve Yates, Alison Parnum and Leslie Cram of Reading Museum Service; Margaret Smith and her colleagues in the Local Studies Section of the Central Reading Library; Jonathan Farmer, photographer; and the Reading Newspaper Company.

BRITAIN IN OLD PHOTOGRAPHS

SUTTON'S PHOTOGRAPHIC HISTORY OF TRANSPORT

To order any of these titles please telephone our distributor, Littlehampton Book Services on 01903 828800
For a catalogue of these and our other titles please ring Emma Leitch on 01453 731114